Amazing Daisy

"Coloured Bedtime StoryBook"

By

Leona Ingram

&

Nozizwe Herero

Illustrated by

Siya Masuku

ILLUSTRATED & PUBLISHED
BY
E-KİTAP PROJESİ & CHEAPEST BOOKS

www.cheapestboooks.com

www.facebook.com/EKitapProjesi

Copyright, 2024 by e-Kitap Projesi
Istanbul

ISBN: 978-625-6308-55-8

Categories: Adventure, Community
Country of Origin: United States
Cover: © Cheapest Books
License: CC-BY-4.0

For full terms of use and attribution, http://creativecommons.org/licenses/by/4.0/

Narrator: Dunlop

© **All rights reserved**.

Except for the conditions stated in the License, no part of this book shall be reproduced or transmitted in any form or by any means, electronic or mechanical, including photocopy, recording or by any information or retrieval system, without written permission form the publisher.

About the Book

Daisy wants to fly but all of the other chickens laugh at her and tell her that chickens can't fly. Will Daisy fly?

[4]

Once upon a time on a little farm near a little village…

...there lived a little chicken called Daisy.

"When I grow up, I want to fly high, high into the sky," Daisy said.

But all the other chickens laughed at her.

"You are so weird," they said. "We won't play with you anymore."

"Daisy, we can all flap our wings but it's very difficult for chickens to fly," Mama told her.

Daisy wouldn't give up. Every day she practised by herself, flapping her wings. Flap, flap, flap, she would flap her wings but she couldn't lift off the ground.

While she practised, she imagined herself flying high into the sky and looking at the chickens below. She imagined herself flying past the sparrows and past the swallows. "Wow!" the birds would say. "A chicken that can fly!"

So ... Flap, flap, flap, every day Daisy would flap her wings.

She would lift off the ground but fall down again.

"I'm never going to fly!" Daisy cried to Mama. "The others are right." "Daisy, you are different from the other chickens. They don't want to fly but you do! You can do it," Mama said.

The following day Daisy climbed to the top of the chicken coop and flap, flap, flap, she flapped her wings. She flew into the air and flapped her wings ... and flapped her wings ... and flapped her wings and ...

The other chickens laughed out loud. "Ha ha ha! We told you! Chickens can't fly!"

But the next day Daisy climbed even higher, right up to the top of the rondavel. Flap, flap, flap, Daisy flapped her wings.

She flew into the air and flapped her wings ... and flapped her wings ... and flapped her wings and ...

She kept flying! The wind beneath her wings grew stronger and she flew higher and higher! The sparrows and the swallows said, "Amazing! A flying chicken!"

And the other chickens wanted to be just like her. They said, "Oh Daisy, you're amazing!"

End of the Story

www.ingramcontent.com/pod-product-compliance
Lightning Source LLC
LaVergne TN
LVHW070454080526
838202LV00035B/2825